THE ART of

de-stressing

REMOVING THE MOST STRESSFUL OBSTACLES TO PERSONAL AND PROFESSIONAL SUCCESS

RAY H. HULL, PHD

Published and Distributed by
SOUND WISDOM
PO Box 310
Shippensburg, PA 17257-0310
717-530-2122
info@soundwisdom.com
www.soundwisdom.com

ISBN 13: 978-1-64095-392-5
ISBN 13 eBook: 978-1-64095-393-2

For Worldwide Distribution, Printed in the U.S.A.
1 2 3 4 5 6 / 26 25 24 23 22

TABLE OF CONTENTS

Achieving Success in Your Personal and Professional Life

This book contains 20 lessons that, if read and taken to heart, will assist you in becoming more successful in your personal and professional life. As my dear friend and four-time coauthor Jim Stovall has said so well, "Each of us is born with unlimited potential and unlimited options. When we are born, it is almost as if we were born with a banner that proclaims, 'I'm lovable, I'm capable, and I'm able to do anything I set my mind to.'"[1] We can be successful in anything we set our mind to!

Have you ever watched a young child dance to music? They smile; they dance in a most uninhibited manner! They are a prime example of "I can do anything well! I can dance, I can sing, I can laugh out loud, and everyone applauds! I am loved! I'm wonderful!" Those children are examples of undaunted success! As far as they are concerned, they can do anything well!

But then, as we enter school and then college and eventually our professional life, we tend to lose the confidence that we once had as a child. Our confidence in our ability to be successful in whatever we decide to do with our lives becomes clouded. We're not as sure of our abilities, our knowledge, or our talent. Where did we lose our confidence? We were probably not told by our parents, our teachers, or our colleagues that we could be successful in our life. Instead, we were told that we were not as good or talented as we thought that we were or could be. As we grew up, we did not receive the same praise as we did in early childhood.

I have been awarded enumerable citations and awards during my professional life; authored over 70 highly recognized professional journal articles and 28 well-received books published by major publishing companies; made over 600 major presentations at conferences and conventions across the United States, Canada, Europe, and South America; and have received other forms of recognition during my professional life. However, an example of what can be done to downgrade one's own opinion of their potential for success in their professional life came from one of my professors during my undergraduate degree program. He is one of those you never forget, not because of his scholarship, encouragement, and praise, but because of his negativity. I took a required course in American History taught by that professor. During one class period, we were to take one of three examinations. The professor was walking down the aisle where I was sitting at my desk, and I was glancing at a few of my notes to remind myself of some items that I thought might be on the test. As he approached my desk, I quickly put my notes and textbook away. He looked down and said calmly but with great negativity, "There is *nothing* in those notes or that book that will help you, Mr. Hull!"

That, of course, was one of the worst and most demeaning things that any professor could say to one of his students! I was demoralized and terribly hurt by what he said to me. However, I rose above what that professor said and also what my high school advisor said when he remarked that I should never become a teacher due to my stuttering. By rising above those negative predictions, I completed my PhD in neuroscience at a prestigious university and have since become an award-winning professor, author, and public speaker.

During her middle school and high school years, our daughter Courtney was told by her advisor that after graduating from high school she might be able to complete the requirements of a technical school but she should not attempt completing a degree program at a college or university. He told her that he didn't feel that she had the intellectual promise to do so. After being given that negative advice, Courtney came home that day quite depressed. She had planned to attend one of the local universities in our city to complete her bachelor's degree. After that degree, her dream was to complete a master's degree and then a PhD in order to become a university administrator. However, after her advisor told her of his opinion and recommendation, she felt that perhaps she didn't have the potential to go to college at all.

After being born very prematurely at a mere 1 pound, 11 ounces, and struggling throughout her young life to catch up to her peers both physically and intellectually, Courtney rose above her advisor's opinion. She has graduated with her bachelor's degree in strategic communication as an honors student in the prestigious Elliott School of Communication at Wichita State University, and she is completing her master's degree in the same concentration as an honors student with a straight-A average in that same school and university. She certainly has risen above the negative predictions with all her accolades, and so can you!

This book is written to give you, the reader, an understanding of how anyone can be a success! It provides 20 insights into the process of being successful as you enter into any endeavor or relationship. I hope that you enjoy this book and, as you read it, discover avenues for success that perhaps you had not conceived of before.

Take this book and devour it! It could become your partner in success within your professional and personal life!

CHAPTER 1

Why Are You Here?

*W*e all want to achieve success in our personal and professional life. Of course, there are different levels of success and different interpretations of what is contained in a definition of success. The meaning of success for one person may be different for another individual. For one person, success may center on money—to make as much money as possible. For another, success may mean a family where love abounds. For another, it may be achieving success in their occupation, no matter what the income might be. There are probably as many definitions of success as there are people who strive to achieve it!

How do we achieve this thing called "success," and what exactly is it? Here are some suggestions:

First of all, according to Dr. Sherrie Campbell, author of the book *Success Equations*, it is necessary to *be authentic*—to be yourself.[2] If we try to change our personality to fit various occasions or different customers, it doesn't work because we are attempting to be someone we are not.

She also recommends that we *be truthful.* There is nothing greater that we can offer than to be honest in all that we do. We then achieve trust.

Third, we should *treat all others with dignity and value.* It is important to cause those with whom we associate to feel that they are cared for and important. To love all others in our life is a quality that seems to be rare nowadays, but it is one that will lead to love and respect in return.

If you feel that you are being held back from where you will find success, *identify the barriers.* If it is fear, it is important to go beyond the emotion of fear and focus on the positive—to take the risk that you *can* indeed succeed! Norman Vincent Peale has said so many times that if we think positively about ourselves and our potential, we can go beyond fear into our own realm of success!

Kathy Caprino advocates for the importance of developing the ability to *communicate effectively.* Success is built on the ability to communicate powerfully—to speak in such a way that we inspire others who will support us and our successes. Caprino also says that successful professionals know how to negotiate and advocate for themselves in exciting ways without putting others off.[3]

Remember, in asking the question, "What is success, and how can I achieve it?" the only person who can answer that question is *you*. I have not been able to locate a definitive definition of success or how to achieve that goal. Everyone has differing opinions on what it is and how to achieve it. In the end, we must define it for ourselves.

IF WE DON'T ACHIEVE SUCCESS, DID WE FAIL?

If we cannot truly define "success," then can we define "failure"? As the multimillionaire Malcolm Forbes has said so well, "Failure is success if we learn from it."[4] It has been said that Thomas Edison's attempts at developing a prototype of the light bulb failed at least 1,000 times.

When he was asked how it felt to fail that many times, he replied that he didn't fail at all. He said that developing the light bulb simply required 1,000 steps before achieving success. That is a wonderful way to conceptualize success.

We decide what success means to us, we learn from our mistakes, and we commit to moving toward our goal—the goal that defines our success. And if we fail at achieving that goal, rather than thinking that it is the end of the world, we pick ourselves up, we learn from our failures, and we move forward!

CHAPTER 2

How to Handle Everyday Stress with Poise

I received a phone call from a young woman about a week ago who wanted to ask me about communicating in meetings. She said that she has a difficult time maintaining her composure during staff meetings. She said that when something she has said in a staff meeting is challenged by a colleague, she tries very hard to remain calm and respond in a professional manner. However, she sometimes "loses it" during the discussion, raises her voice, and is embarrassed about it later. She said that it distresses her that during staff meetings some of her colleagues are somehow able to goad her into becoming so stressed that she loses her poise and falls apart in front of everyone.

As we talked, a quote that Jim Stovall and I shared in one of our books, *The Art of Influence*, came to mind. So, I shared it with her. It is, "Calmness is the rarest quality in human life."[5]

She said that may be easy for some people, but she wanted more—she wanted some specifics on how to maintain her poise in stressful situations. So, I offered her something that Dr. Sherrie Campbell, clinical psychologist and expert on mastering poise, has recommended: Whenever you are in any working group, or a position of responsibility, or seeing one of your clients and their family, one way to remain composed is to remember that you always have an audience. Your audience includes your team members, your colleagues, or your clients. They are your audience, and they expect a certain level of calm, serenity, integrity, and grit from you.[6]

I told her that she can literally be an example of calm and poise. I said that one way is to think of herself as being an example of what her colleagues would like to become when faced with stress in their own personal and professional lives. Here are some other recommendations that I shared with her:

Carol Goman, another expert on maintaining poise under pressure, suggests that at the moment in which you are aware that you are in a stressful situation, pause and mentally say the word, "Stop!"[7] Instead of automatically reacting to the event that triggered the stress, you are able to use that pause to gain control and respond with greater poise.

Remember, keeping your poise prevents the stress in the environment from escalating and ensures those around you won't develop a negative attitude toward you.

In a meeting, never take a cheap shot at someone, no matter how good it might make you feel at the moment. You will only regret it later. And apologizing is never fun.

In meetings or in other interpersonal interactions with others, don't make a big deal out of a trivial issue. If you do, ask yourself, "Why am I doing this? What is it that I am after?"

If someone treats you in an unkind manner, practice forgiving, forgetting, and moving on. As one of my favorite colleagues used to say, "It, too, shall pass."

And if you see an argument on the horizon, become a good listener instead. Let the other person vent while you listen quietly. You will win many an "argument" that way, and you won't find yourself in the middle of a potentially embarrassing situation. In other words, when one person says something that might provoke a negative response or an argument, it is best simply to listen quietly, no matter how much you would like to enter the fray!

Remember—you will never get into trouble by admitting that you may be wrong. During a discussion in a meeting, if you realize what the other person is saying is correct and find to your dismay that what you have been advocating is probably wrong, even though we sometimes don't want to admit it, there's nothing wrong with letting go of our ego and saying, "You know, in thinking about it, I believe that you are absolutely right!" That simple response can stop a negative debate or an embarrassing situation in its tracks, and it makes everyone feel better.

Poise under pressure is an art. It is an art that we purposely develop. We certainly are not born with the poise to maintain calm in stressful situations. Have you ever observed a three-year-old child in a restaurant who remains calm when their toy is taken away by a family member because he or she was banging it on the table? I never have! In fact, some adults never seem to develop the ability to remain calm when they are under stress. It is definitely not a trait that is inherently ingrained in people. It is a trait that we must learn in order to function well in the world.

We need to know when to let something go. If we find ourselves in a stressful discussion and cannot come to an agreement, sometimes it is best simply to agree to disagree. If a discussion is going nowhere, it might be appropriate to disengage and move on. And in moving on, we can still shake hands and appreciate the other person, even if we don't agree!

Those were the suggestions that I not only gave her but also sent to her in a letter as well. I hope they helped. They have helped me!

A final word—in our professional life, it is best to become the person we would like to be. I like to call it developing the art of "positive vulnerability"—that is, becoming transparent in our dealings with our team members and leaders—revealing ourselves first as people who care deeply for them. This is the "poise" or "charm" that causes others to want to work with us because they know that we are who we are and we can be trusted as professionals to do our very best on their behalf without pretense, without argument, and without stress.

CHAPTER 3

How to Achieve What You Want to Achieve in Your Personal and Professional Life

Consistency counts! I was reading a post the other day by Carly Benson on her blog *Miracles are Brewing*, and some of her thoughts caught my eye. She said that getting good at something and achieving success in whatever it might be requires consistent work and repetition. She continued by saying that consistency is not only important, but it is essential in order to achieve success.[8]

I like what she said. For example, in regard to my own life, I have always wanted to play the piano well—to play in such a way that I could sit down at the piano at parties or other such events and impress the others who were in attendance. The same goes for the guitar. But my dedication to long-term practice was not consistent over time, and so my success at playing the piano and the guitar has suffered.

We cannot learn something new or become an expert at something by working at it for short periods of time and then letting it become dormant. Consistency is what counts—it is an absolute must for success.

Jim Stovall says that long-term success at anything is achieved and enjoyed by average people who perform consistently over a long period of time. He says that whenever you hear of someone becoming an overnight success, it is likely that they were working for years behind the scenes and their success has just come to the public's attention.

He states further that if you examine studies of self-made millionaires, the overwhelming majority compiled their wealth over many years and formed lifelong habits of spending less than they earned and investing wisely and consistently. Someone asked him the question, "How come there are so many people offering quick-fix solutions for making money, losing weight, staying healthy, and becoming successful?" He said the reason is very simple: it is that the reality of working long and hard to achieve those accomplishments— staying focused, being diligent, and being consistent in working to gain them—isn't attractive and doesn't sell well in infomercials on cable television. That's why!

Being consistent in our efforts to achieve success, whether it is in business or playing the piano, is the cornerstone of being who you were meant to be. It is what counts in the long run.

Consistency doesn't mean trying for one day and giving up, nor does it mean doing the same thing wrong repeatedly in exactly the same way. What it does mean is not only doing what you have found to be successful over and over again, but also working to improve it on a regular basis. It takes focus, motivation, and dedication.

Consistency means making sure that the steps you are taking toward your goals are not ones that are simply wasting your time—in other words, avoiding steps that have nothing to do with moving you closer to what you are trying to achieve.

It means staying motivated about achieving your goals. If we are not motivated, we will never maintain consistency in working toward them. We will be wasting our time and energy.

In the end, being consistent in working toward our goals means that we feel encouraged that we are actually moving forward—we feel happy. And unless we're happy, we won't be successful in achieving our goals.

CHAPTER 4

How to Bounce Back from Troubling Times

There are times in both our personal and professional lives that are emotionally draining. Our offices and our homes can become busy and hectic. There can be distractions that take away our creativity and our ability to concentrate on matters that need to be taken care of. At times it can be challenging to make rational decisions that are needed, to concentrate on tasks at hand, and to maintain our composure.

There are also times when we must deal with loss. It could be divorce, the loss of a job, or other stresses that cause us to feel that the world is crumbling around us. To help us deal with those times, we all need a place where we can shift our inner being for even a few minutes to focus, solve problems, and cleanse our mind.

So, we all need our own special quiet place—a place where we can problem-solve, meditate, and regenerate.

I grew up on farms in the center of Kansas. I had my own special place where I could reflect, regroup, search for answers, and talk things out that were bothering me where no one could hear me. With my dog, Laddie, I would walk about one-half of a mile diagonally across one of our fields to a place where the house and outbuildings of an old farmstead once stood. The house, barn, and outbuildings had been demolished long ago, and all that remained were three tall elm trees and a mound of dirt that partially covered what used to be the family's cellar. The old stone stairway to the cellar was still there, but it was mostly filled with dirt. I never took the time to work my way down into that old stairway because I don't care for spiders. But my special place was under those three trees that were once in the front yard of that old house.

I would sit quietly with my dog in the shade of the trees and regain a sense of calm. Out in that wheat field, I was away from everything and everybody. No one could see me because of the undergrowth. The only sound came from the wind and the rustling of the leaves on those three old elm trees. The leaves produced a wonderfully lonely sound. Nothing else could be heard.

That was my special place, my sanctuary away from the rest of the world, where I could think, problem-solve, meditate, rekindle my awareness that everything in my life was going to be okay and that God was still in Heaven. My quiet place helped me grow into early manhood away from the distractions of a busy world.

We all need our own special place. It may not be in the corner of a wheat field, but it can be a corner of your office or your home where there is a picture or a window view that is calming to you—one you can look at and dream a little, clear your mind when your world seems to be falling apart, problem-solve, and regenerate. I have three framed pictures in my office that show beautiful mountains and a lake that look very much like the places my good friend Bob and I would go fishing for trout when I lived in Colorado. They are calming to me. And when I must do some problem-solving or I need to cleanse my mind, closing the door to my office and gazing at those mountains and lakes allows me a few moments to resolve issues that must be resolved, to reach rational decisions, to meditate, and to experience a sense of renewal.

I find, then, that problem-solving and the creation of new ideas come easier. Sometimes just those few moments of silence and reflection can do wonders—bringing peace of mind and a few moments of calm to times that would otherwise be stressful.

We all need our own special place—a quiet place where we can reflect, create, and bounce back from troubling times.

CHAPTER 5

How to Find Your Own Special Talent

*A*fter my previous writings on the topic of success in one's professional life, I have received several questions via email. The one that required some in-depth research on my part was as follows: "Is a special talent required in order to achieve real success?"

Here is what I have found that responds directly to that question. The answer is probably a qualified "no." However, it is impossible to disprove that some natural talent doesn't exist in extremely successful people. On the other hand, it could be that some people have a "knack" for certain things; and if you find something for which you have a certain knack, you will probably succeed at it. We might think, "I wish I had so and so's talent. I wish my stars were lined up like hers or his." As Patrick Allan writes, "Well, the alignment of your stars can change. You just have to be the one to change them!"[9]

We might think, *I'll never be that good because I just don't have the talent.* We assume that we must have an innate talent to do something well. As soon as you begin to think that, however, you have already denied yourself the chance to succeed. Success is born from passion, dedication, and the belief that you can succeed! That boils down to one word: *confidence!* With confidence, we can develop our own talents. With confidence, we can dedicate ourselves to achieving our goals, whatever they may be.

So, how do we develop the talent that will bring us to the level of success we want to reach? I already mentioned two crucial elements, but to elaborate they are:

CONFIDENCE

Confidence is the inner belief that you can deliver what is required to get a job done well. Confidence is not gained by "charisma" or securing approval from others. Confidence is believing in your own ability and, from that place of self-assurance, showing people that you are the right person to achieve a given task.

MOTIVATION

Motivation is our drive to get things done. You are moving toward your goals; you are committed to achieving them.

Some people wonder whether it takes talent or fortitude to succeed in achieving one's goals—whether a drive to succeed can really match natural aptitude. When we were in school, most of us knew someone who never seemed to have to study hard to achieve good grades while we, on the other hand, had to study hard to achieve grades that never seemed to match theirs. All through college we had to study well into the wee hours to pass tough courses, while they seemed to sail through without much effort. We were motivated to make above-average grades, and we had to work hard to achieve them. They, on the other hand, seemed to have the intelligence, or the "talent," that allowed them to relax and watch the rest of us struggle.

Who do you feel was most successful in their chosen occupation after graduation? It certainly wasn't those who never seemed to have to work hard to achieve their goals. It was those who were motivated to work hard to achieve them!

Is it talent or hard work? Hard work, confidence, and motivation are what pay off in the end!

CHAPTER 6

How to Ace the Personal Pitch

*T*he other day I received a phone call from a young woman who sounded worried and anxious. She had questions regarding an interview she was to engage in for a rather prestigious position with a Fortune 500 company. Her questions centered on difficulties that she was expecting during the interview. She doubted her ability to speak effectively in front of a group. She was only 22 years of age and had just graduated from college with a major in business administration and a minor in entrepreneurship. She imagined that those who would be asking her questions during the interview would probably be her senior by a number of years, and she was concerned that she would feel intimidated and would be unable to handle their questions. She felt that the opportunities offered through that Fortune 500 company were so numerous that she wanted to prepare as best she could for the interview.

Here's what I told her. I said that if she follows these rules for making a compelling personal pitch, she should do very well during her interview:

The most important thing to remember is to try very hard to remain calm and collected, even if you begin to forget your pitch or feel as though you are being overwhelmed with questions.

Always practice your pitch ahead of time, saying it different ways each time so that you communicate coherently and confidently without sounding robotic. For an interview, you might not be able to anticipate every question, but you can be sure they will ask you about your experience and why you are interested in the position.

Always make eye contact with your audience to convey self-assurance and to maintain their engagement. In an interview, when you enter the room (virtual or otherwise) where your interview will take place, pause, smile, and take time to greet each member of the interview team individually. Even if it takes a few moments, it will impress the team if you make good eye contact and tell them all how pleased you are that you have been invited to be interviewed.

Always keep your responses to questions concise, and do not give more information than was requested. Speakers can find themselves in trouble by continuing to talk after they have answered a question, thinking that perhaps they have not said enough.

Never look at your watch or phone!

Never ask about salary in an interview! If the interviewers feel comfortable revealing salary details, they will tell you.

Never simply walk into the room and quietly sit down. You will not impress anyone by being the "timid soul." That's not the way to connect with your audience.

Never look panicked or bewildered. That's difficult to do sometimes, but that is where becoming a good *actor* can be important. If you cannot think of a response to a question, it's fine to appear contemplative or to ask for a restatement of the question in different terms. It may give you time to compose your response. Don't respond to multiple sub-questions contained in a single lengthy question. Separate them and respond only to those about which you feel most comfortable.

If you cannot answer a question directly, it's appropriate to relate it to a similar issue or situation that you feel more confident addressing. Remember—no one expects you to have excellent answers to every question. There is no shame in saying an honest, "I'm not sure, but I will be pleased to respond later after I have had time to think about it."

After your pitch has concluded, once again smile, stand, remain poised, and thank your audience.

Delivering a personal pitch, especially in the context of an interview, is seldom a comfortable situation. But if you follow these suggestions, you should not fail. You can make a generally uncomfortable situation into one that is a winner!

CHAPTER 7

How to Handle Difficult People

During my workshops on the topic of "The Art of Communication in Professional Life," I am frequently asked by members of the audience about my opinion on how they can deal effectively with difficult people in their organizations. That is a very difficult area because there are so many varieties of difficult people who possess vastly different personalities, and the circumstances in which they interact with others can also vary just as greatly. If every difficult person had the same personality and worked in the same environment, then the complexities that exist in dealing with them would be fewer.

Here are six tips that can assist you in the task of communicating with difficult people regardless of the environment or scenario:

KEEP YOUR COOL

The first rule in communicating with difficult people is to maintain your composure. The less reactive you are, the more you can use your better judgment to handle challenging situations. Use the old-fashioned, sage advice that my mother gave to me: "Hold your breath and count to ten." During that span of time, you may figure out a way to handle the situation in a productive manner.

DON'T GET DRAGGED INTO A VERBAL FIGHT

Make sure that you are aware of who the "troublemakers" are in the organization, and don't let them suck you into their world of negativity. Always keep your guard up and remain cool. Never enter a verbal fray, even if you are convinced that you have all of the right answers. Wait until the right moment to assert yourself after the "troublemaker" has exhausted what he or she has intended to say.

PICK YOUR BATTLES

Remember, many difficult people also have positive qualities. We just need to know how to bring out those positive qualities. Being nice to the person while ignoring their outbursts is just one method, and then saying something like, "Remember during our last meeting when you came up with that great idea about…" will likely discourage negative comments from being made.

IGNORE NEGATIVE COMMENTS THAT ARE DIRECTED AT YOU

Negative comments directed at you are often intended to dominate or intimidate you. Typically, those who make them are quick to point out that there is something not right with you or how you do things. Their focus is on "what's wrong," rather than on how to resolve a problem. A simple and powerful way to change this is to put the spotlight back onto the difficult person. The easiest way to do this is to ask them questions without being self-depreciating, e.g., "Then tell me, what can be done to make this situation better? Can you think of one thing that can be done? You often have good ideas, so I would like to hear them."

USE APPROPRIATE HUMOR

You can disarm unreasonable and difficult behavior by using some humor. It shows your detachment, and it allows you to avoid being reactive to the behavior.

REMEMBER THAT IT'S NOT ABOUT WINNING

Some people seem to thrive on arguments, and they like to "win." There are no winners in an argument. Generally, one person simply gives up when they realize that the argument isn't going anywhere. Remember, it takes two to keep an argument going.

If your discussion or argument isn't going anywhere, then you can simply agree to disagree and go on with your life. You can still respect the other person and move on to constructive issues. We must remember that everyone has their own agenda, and they approach discussions regarding what they feel is important in their own way. Rather than discussions, those can evolve into arguments if we allow them to. Our job is to try our best to enter those discussions with an open mind. If we approach the other person with our own set agenda on how to deal with their arguments, what could have been a constructive discussion may devolve into a verbal battle. Our best approach is to be a good listener, hear what the other person has to say with an open mind, and remain calm and collected as we enter the discussion.

CHAPTER 8

How to Create Opportunity

7o some it appears that very successful people always seem to be in the right place at the right time—thus their success. "So why," we ask, "can't that happen to me?"

According to Jim Stovall, if you "peel back the layers of success of successful people," it becomes apparent that success is generally not an accident or a random occurrence.[10] Successful people aren't simply lucky to find themselves in the right place when opportunity knocks. Rather, it takes planning, preparation, knowledge, and, importantly, a willingness to act on an opportunity when one opens up to them!

Chris Riotta gives a prime example of jumping at an opportunity that turns out to be life-changing. He tells of Ryan Graves, who was 26 years old when he tweeted "Hire me?" to Travis Kalanick, who was searching on Twitter for a fellow entrepreneur to get in on the beginning of a start-up. The startup was Uber. Because of his quick "Hire me?" tweet, Graves was Uber's first hire and has now officially joined the *Forbes* Billionaire List along with Uber cofounder Garrett Camp!

Riotta continues by saying that perhaps Graves was lucky when he happened to spot the tweet that would change his life. But it wasn't just that he happened to spot the tweet, it is what he *did* with it that counts—how he seized a small and obscure opportunity that has made him one of the world's youngest billionaires![11]

Dan Waldschmidt stresses that "being in the right place at the right time is really a lesson in persistence."[12] He emphasizes that if you haven't yet achieved the goal that you had set out for yourself, you shouldn't think that your goal is silly or impossible and give up. You should simply remind yourself that perhaps today isn't the right time to achieve your goal. Maybe tomorrow is, because tomorrow might just be the day you find yourself standing "in the right place at the right time"! When that happens, the frustration you have felt will fade away in the glory of finding that it's all worth it!

We all have amazing access to information today. We can acquire immediate details about the latest business trends around the world, but we must remember that these trends are already occurring—and if you try to leap onto the bandwagon, you will be chasing the crowd, and chasing the crowd is never a good method for achieving success. Instead, we should look at all the information that is available and ask ourselves the critical questions about how it relates to what we desire to achieve. *How does it relate to my desired success—my destiny—what I want in my life?*

If you can master the information around you, practice patience and good judgment, and act when the opportunity is right, you will find yourself in the right place at the right time, doing the right thing! People will look at you and talk about how lucky you are!

CHAPTER 9

How to Deliver a Great Presentation

*N*early everyone, at one time or another, is asked to stand before an audience to "say a few words," perhaps to give a presentation on a new product, a new method of service delivery, or another matter. The fear of public speaking can be awful. *What if what I say doesn't make sense? What if I stand before the audience and freeze and I can't talk? What if I stand there and look foolish? What if…* The fear can go on and on! In fact, research has consistently shown that greater than the fear of heights, bugs, snakes, drowning, flying, or ghosts is the fear of speaking in public!

REMEMBER, THE ROOM IS YOUR CANVAS— YOURS ALONE!

You are the artist. The stage or meeting room is your canvas. What you do with it is up to you. You can "wow" your audience by creating a masterpiece, or you can put them to sleep. Which do you choose?

IT ISN'T NECESSARY TO CREATE A MASTERPIECE

It isn't necessary to create a masterpiece, but we can create something that is acceptable, something that is good, and something that is liked. It doesn't have to be perfect. I have given well over 800 presentations at conferences and conventions around the world over the past 20 years. Occasionally, I am asked to give three or four presentations over a period of a day or two. The most I have given was three consecutive one-hour presentations. By the third hour, I had to do my best to bring myself up and say with enthusiasm, "It is GREAT to be here!"—and mean it!

WE MUST PREPARE OURSELVES

So, we must *prepare* ourselves to feel comfortable in front of an audience. That means placing ourselves in front of an audience, whether we want to or not, because we said we would! We look for ways to practice our stage presence and speaking ability in non-threatening environments. Those can include:

- Making announcements at meetings or social gatherings

- Reading minutes or sharing reports in the meetings you attend

- Volunteering to introduce a guest speaker

- Joining and participating in Toastmasters International

- Giving a brief presentation at your next business meeting

There are additional ways through which we can develop confidence in the area of public speaking. For example, Dale Carnegie public speaking classes are a wonderful way to practice public speaking in an environment of people who are just like you! For example, I was a severe stutterer throughout high school and college. Thinking that it might help, my parents enrolled me in a Dale Carnegie public speaking course in our hometown that met once a week for six weeks. By the time the six weeks concluded, my speech was nearly fluent, and I was rated as one of the best public speakers in my class! That six-week course did more good for my ability to speak than most anything else that had been tried over the years. I am now a sought-after public speaker and an award-winning university professor!

WHAT DOES IT TAKE TO BE A CONFIDENT PRESENTER?

It takes...

ENTHUSIASM

Confident presenters exude enthusiasm. If the presenter doesn't look and sound enthusiastic, why should anyone else be enthusiastic about it?

ENGAGING THE AUDIENCE

Confident presenters do everything in their power to engage each member of the audience. Look at the audience and make eye contact individually with as many members as you can!

A TAKE-CHARGE ATTITUDE

Confident presenters take charge! They look poised. They sound prepared. Their goal is simply to persuade, influence, or inform.

A NATURAL STYLE

A confident presenter's style is natural. Their delivery has a conversational feel. Confident presenters make it look easy. They appear comfortable with the audience.

OWNING THE ROOM

One way to become a convincing speaker is to "own the room," which involves "working" the stage with absolute confidence. Owning the room comes from an open communication style—immediately assessing what the audience needs and expects and delivering it with gusto.

Effective public speaking takes practice, it takes a natural style of speaking, it takes confidence, and it takes stage presence! You can do it!

CHAPTER 10

How to Take Control of Your Day

*W*hen I observe others who always seem to be on top of things, I become a little envious. They seem to nearly always be ahead of schedule in completing tasks that are required of them. They seem to have an almost intuitive sense of what needs to be done—and when. I admire those individuals for their ability to "get things done"! I think that most of us know a few people like that. They don't seem to be the ones who take work home with them. They don't work late at the office. They take weekends off to be with family and tell us on Monday what a great time they had. But yet they seem to be able to get all of their work completed on time, and when given additional tasks to do, they seem to complete them with ease.

That's when I think of my father and how he managed a complex farming operation. He was a wonderful example of "getting it done." Here's the story:

As I have mentioned, I was born and raised on our farms in the middle of the state of Kansas. It amounted to three farms considered to be one farming operation. Obviously, there was a lot to do to maintain the entire operation that included three sizeable grain operations, a 75-cow dairy, a 1,000-head feeder pig operation, row crops, alfalfa, wheat, and beef cattle. The totality of the organization and its management was on the shoulders of one man—my father.

Growing up, I was his main hired hand during my grade school, high school, and college years, and I was also in charge of making sure our two or three hired hands were completing their tasks. My primary responsibilities revolved around morning and evening chores of feeding calves, making sure the cows had fresh hay and fresh water, and more. The thing I most enjoyed about all of those chores and the field work was when it was finished, it was done! When I finished plowing a field or working a field with the spring tooth, I would stop the tractor and look back over the field to make sure that it was complete. If it was and it looked good, my work there was finished! It was a good feeling to look back over that field and to know that the job was done and that it looked good!

That's the problem with so many other occupations that we find ourselves involved in today. It seems that frequently there are so many things that need to be done—and at nearly the same time—that we wonder if we will ever complete them. Nothing ever seems to be finished!

I was reading a book recently that was written by David Allen entitled *Getting Things Done: Stress-Free Productivity*.[13] He gives some good suggestions on how to prioritize, organize, and get things done! I'm paraphrasing here, but what he says is very much akin to what my father did to maintain a well-organized farming operation. Here are a few suggestions:

MAKE A LIST

Write a to-do list by hand on a pad of paper. Don't keep a list of what needs to be accomplished in your head! That gives one a false sense of control regarding all that needs to be done.

Remember, if you don't complete a task before you leave for the day, you haven't failed. It will be waiting for you tomorrow morning when you arrive at work.

Reflect on your to-do list by breaking it down into workable steps so that the list doesn't overwhelm you.

Be sure to ask yourself, "What am I trying to do, and why?" Is it important that No. 4 on your list be completed now? Can it wait for a little bit while you make sure that No. 3 is absolutely complete to the best of your ability? Making those decisions can be frustrating, but it is far better to make those decisions about the absolute importance of the tasks on your list. Not making those decisions causes us to remain in our daily "busy" mode. We look busy, but are we accomplishing much?

How did my father manage his very complex farming operation all by himself? He did it by way of organization. He was impeccably well organized, and he lived by his lists of what needed to be done and when.

SET PRIORITIES

Setting your priorities is another critically important part of getting things done. We say, "Oh my! Where do I begin?"

There seems to be no end to the advice that is available to us on the topic of setting priorities. We develop charts, graphs, boards covered with sticky notes, and other mechanisms to help us set our goals that need to be accomplished. As time passes, however, those practices are generally cast aside. Setting our priorities for each day shouldn't be that complicated. We can make a list that includes:

(1) What do I absolutely have to accomplish—by today? by the end of this week?

(2) When is it absolutely required to be completed?

(3) Do I have what it takes to accomplish it by myself, or do I need help?

If your highest-priority task needs to be completed by the end of the day, barring phone calls and other interruptions, try breaking the task down into individual parts. Take a deep breath and begin working on the first part. After completing that element, take a short break before starting on the second part. Take another break after you finish that task, pausing also to appreciate what you have accomplished thus far, and then tackle the next step—or, if timing does not allow for it, plan how you will complete it tomorrow.

DON'T TAKE YOUR PROJECTS HOME WITH YOU

There used to be a way to ensure we didn't constantly feel a need to do more. It was called "going home." However, with the advent of new technology, we can now work from anywhere, and so leaving the office doesn't necessarily mean "leaving work." While working constantly seems to have become a new "normal" for many, common sense says that working constantly and doing well in what we are trying to accomplish is unsustainable. Even though it's tempting to try, in the end it just doesn't work!

CHAPTER 11

How to Deal with Incivility

*L*ately there has been a flurry of news and conversation on the topic of civility and respect in professional settings. It's a topic whose importance has been downplayed for too long. In a study published in the *Journal of Occupational Health Psychology*, in a survey of 1,100 workers, 781 had experienced workplace incivility.[14] According to S. Chris Edmonds in "The Little Black Book of Billionaire Secrets," which appeared in the *Forbes Community Voice* in 2016, 62 percent of employees had been treated rudely at work at least once a month.[15] The rudeness had come from coworkers and/or their superiors.

If we could define the term "civility," it would include the following:

CIVILITY INVOLVES SHOWING RESPECT TOWARD OTHERS

People are not objects, nor are they simply opportunities for advancement. When we treat others with respect, we are treating them as we would likewise appreciate being treated. We ensure that they do not feel like an inconvenience but rather that their ideas are welcome.

When someone meets with you, they will make an appraisal of your attitude, your mood, your intentions, and your feelings about them within two minutes. A smile, a friendly nod, and an outstretched hand to indicate that they are about to enter a supportive conversation is what they are hoping for. If instead they receive a frustrated frown, a downward look, and a growl to "be seated," they will suddenly move into survival mode and expect the worst!

CIVILITY CAUSES OTHERS TO FEEL GOOD ABOUT BEING IN THAT ENVIRONMENT

Civility enables people to know that they are in an inclusive work environment where each individual is valued for the contributions they make to the organization. They know that their leaders work based on facts rather than assumptions or gossip. Individuals are shown that they are valued, and as an important part of a team they feel free to contribute to the organization in the best way that they can. They know they won't be reprimanded for their efforts if they do not turn out as well as they thought they would.

Rather, they will be complimented for the work that they accomplish for the team.

CIVILITY REQUIRES EFFECTIVE INTERPERSONAL COMMUNICATION

Interpersonal communication is an ongoing process with everyone—that means everyone in the organization, not just those closest to the leader. Those with whom we communicate should feel a connection to us. They know that we care about them and support them.

It is important to remember that the nonverbal aspects of communication comprise more than 70 percent of what is being communicated. That means the words that we use comprise only about 30 percent of what is being said. The nonverbal aspects of communication are powerful and include eye contact, body language, gestures, vocal inflections, and intonation. Civility therefore demands that we are respectful and affirming in our nonverbal communication as much as in the words we speak.

Leaning too far forward with shoulders hunched or slouching indicates that you, the listener, have decided against what is being said. Leaning too far back in a chair with your hand covering your mouth indicates hostility toward the speaker's ideas or skepticism about their line of reasoning. That may not be intended, but that is what your nonverbals are saying. And that impression is difficult to erase.

Standing with your arms folded across your chest can also indicate resistance to what is being said, or impatience. Playing with your fingers or nails or engaging in other fidgeting behaviors indicates that you are not really listening to the other person.

Finally, our eyes give us away! Lack of eye contact, or frequent glances to one side or the other, indicates serious disagreement or disinterest.

People are drawn to those who make them feel most comfortable, those who communicate with them in a positive and supportive manner. In the end, it is what separates those who are successful in life and in work from those who are less successful.

CIVILITY MEANS VALUING EVERYONE'S PERSPECTIVE

We welcome a diversity of ideas and perspectives, and no discrimination is allowed based on gender, race, ethnicity, sexual orientation, military status, disability, age, and so on. We listen carefully, with good eye contact and no sideglances. We concentrate on what the other person is saying, with an occasional nod to assure the person that we are listening. And we never look at our watch or phone! We never interrupt. Rather, we reflect on their feelings with supportive attentiveness. In other words, the person knows that she or he is respected and valued and that we are listening.

CIVILITY MEANS HANDLING DISAGREEMENTS AND DELIVERING CRITICISM IN PRIVATE

Reprimanding or criticizing someone in front of others is not acceptable behavior, no matter what the cause or the reason! If someone makes a mistake, we must do whatever is possible to help that person save face. No matter how wrong we might think the person is, we only destroy ego and potentially good working relations by embarrassing the other person and hurting their dignity. And hurting someone's dignity can be extremely damaging to an otherwise positive working relationship. If it is deemed necessary to tell a team member that an error was made and change is necessary, that conversation must occur in private.

The result of a lack of respect and civil behavior toward others, particularly if those behaviors originate from a leader, usually results in team members who are fearful and stressed. Therefore, they don't perform their responsibilities to the potential they would otherwise demonstrate. They will simply "do their job" and leave at the end of the day. The cost in reduced commitment to their organization as a result of anxiety and decreased effort can be extremely high.

How can civility and respect be encouraged? Here are some suggestions:

BE THE ONE TO PROMOTE RESPECT AND CIVILITY

We can be the one who demonstrates respect and civility to others every day. We can consider that to be one of our responsibilities. We accept that responsibility because we feel that it is important for the morale of those in our organization. We can be the example of one who values the contributions of those who work with us. We can compliment and congratulate others when they achieve a goal or accomplish a significant task. However, in the meantime we must not denigrate ourselves by lowering the significance of our own accomplishments. But perhaps in congratulating others for their good work or accomplishments, they will in turn compliment us when we accomplish a significant task or receive an award. Comradery is the goal, and it is refreshing.

INCIVILITY MUST BE IMMEDIATELY ADDRESSED

Many people who are disrespectful of others on either a covert or overt level will not change on their own, primarily because either they cannot see anything wrong with their behavior or they believe that others deserve that behavior. In these instances, it is best to directly address the incivility and ensure the offender knows their behavior is harming the culture. In general, though, we should aim to take care of issues before it is necessary to confront them. A special group meeting that discusses civility and respect at the beginning of the year is quite appropriate. Assure the attendees that the meeting is being held for the purpose of awareness and to encourage comradery in the organization rather than to reprimand. "We are all here to work together, to respect each other, to support each other, to congratulate each other when something has been done well or an award has been received, and to work in a positive and supportive environment." We must emphasize to all team members, no matter what level they are within the organizational structure, that appropriateness in behavior is essential and that inappropriate behavior will be dealt with severely.

Most people desire to treat others as they would like to be treated. However, occurrences of incivility can happen in any environment. Promoting a culture of respect will ensure everyone feels valued and can do their best work.

CHAPTER 12

How to Connect Effectively with Peers and Leaders

*E*ffective communication with our peers and leaders is a critically important part of maintaining morale and a positive attitude within an organization. One avenue that has mushroomed over the past two decades involves the use of email. Another involves constructive listening.

DIGITAL COMMUNICATION

Emails are powerful documents! They can make or break any day for your team members. Email is a wonderful tool for communication, but in today's busy world, it becomes too easy to send a quick, impersonal email rather than taking a few seconds to make it a personal one. And while email is an efficient mode of communication, if misused it can make people feel alienated or offended. I know many who will send an email to a person who is right next to them rather than rising from one's chair and walking a few feet to actually talk! In addition, sometimes people use email to avoid delivering news that should be communicated in person because they don't want to deal with the individual's sadness or discomfort.

Here are some suggestions for the use of emails in professional settings:

When possible, rather than relying totally on email for professional communication, especially when your email is going to only one or two people, use the same amount of time to reach out individually and talk face to face, either in person or via a video call. And before you leave, say something nice to your team member, e.g., "You're doing a great job!"; "I want you to know that I appreciate you and the work you are accomplishing"; "Have a great rest of your day!" A few kind words will make any team member happier to be working with you! The glow produced by those kind words can sometimes do more for productivity than a financial incentive and is certainly more personal than an impersonal email!

Realizing that the sheer number of emails received each day can become burdensome, it is tempting, as the day becomes crowded with other duties, to respond to emails from one's team member or leader in an unintendedly curt manner. We sometimes forget that it takes only a few seconds to respond by using the sender's name, e.g., "Thanks, John, for your email," or "I received your email, Sarah, and I apologize for the delay in responding." Spend an extra eight or so seconds to add a little thoughtfulness and attention to your emails. It shows that you care and that you truly appreciate the efforts of that individual! It works wonders—believe me!

CONSTRUCTIVE LISTENING

Developing the skill of constructive listening is one the most beneficial ways one can connect effectively with team members and leaders and establish a strong working relationship with them. I read a story the other day that clarifies what "listening" involves. It comes from Eugene Raudsepp in his article "The Art of Listening Well." Here it is:

A zoologist was walking down a busy city street with a friend. In the midst of the honking horns and screeching tires, he exclaimed to his friend, "Listen to that cricket!"

The friend looked at the zoologist in astonishment and said, "You hear a cricket in the middle of all this noise and confusion?"

Without a word, the zoologist reached into his pocket, took out a coin, and flipped it into the air. As it clinked on the sidewalk, a dozen heads turned in response.

The zoologist said quietly to his friend, "We hear what we listen for."[16]

Listening is an art that we develop on a conscious level because it is *a critically important part of communication*. We *become* good listeners, not because it is something that is required of us, but because it is something that we need and even want to do well because we care about those who are speaking and/or we are interested in what is being said. We actually participate in the process of communication when we become a good and active listener.

Here are some suggestions on the art of effective listening:

Don't deny the reality of a concern that is being expressed by saying, "Oh...you're making too much out of it" or "You worry too much!" It is best simply to listen carefully and constructively and allow the person to express her or himself freely.

When listening and when asked your opinion about what is being expressed, try diligently to see things from the other person's point of view. Never try to stress *your* point of view over theirs. You are inadvertently negating their opinion in order to indicate that your opinion is correct and theirs is not.

When the other person is expressing their thoughts or concerns, do NOT interject your opinions before the person has finished talking. Even though you feel that you have the solution, interrupting is both inappropriate and disrespectful. It shows that you really didn't care to hear the person's concerns and you wanted to solve the issue quickly so you could go on with whatever you were previously doing.

Give the person who is speaking verbal and nonverbal cues that you are listening. For instance, if the person with whom you are communicating is relaying a sad occurrence in her or his life, show that you are empathetic in your facial expressions and verbal reactions. No side glances! And *never* look at your watch or phone! That's a dead giveaway that you are not really interested in what the other person is saying.

We determine the meaning of what is being said based on our own experiences, so it is important that we ask questions to confirm our understanding—questions such as "Did you mean...?" or "Did I understand you to say...?" go a long way. We can also verify our understanding by paraphrasing or rewording what we heard and asking if what we said is accurate.

We also must pay attention to the nonverbal aspects of what is being said, not just the words that are being spoken. Those include tone of voice and any gestures that are being used. Does the conversation partner appear excited, sad, or confused?

Our own biases and prejudices can become a roadblock to listening. If we have already decided that we do not like or respect the one who is speaking, then listening constructively and with an open mind becomes difficult. Recognizing our biases is important. It gives us a basis for working to get over them. Lisa Marshall notes that "tuning in" is the very first step in achieving any level of effective listening, and it requires us to turn off any mind chatter—erasing anything else we are thinking about and suspending judgment regarding what the speaker is saying.[17] It is important to wait until the other person finishes speaking before forming an opinion or a response.

In conclusion, the effective use of emails and skill in listening can both be considered an art. People are generally not born with good listening skills and are definitely not born with skill in using digital forms of communication. Both are important, and both are learned forms of communication.

Becoming a skilled communicator requires work, self-discipline, and skill. It involves an attention to the words we speak and write as well as the way we listen, and often the latter is the most valuable element of communication. Ask any good salesperson or negotiator about the value of listening in silence, and he or she will tell you that good listeners generally make more sales and better deals. As my mother said to me as I was growing up, "Remember—people like good listeners better than good talkers!"

CHAPTER 13

How to Put Your Career on the Fast Track

If you have wondered about the traits you must have in order to achieve the level of excellence that you desire to reach in your career or business, think in terms of these three: (1) the power of image, (2) the power of enthusiasm, and (3) the power of wisdom.

THE POWER OF PROFESSIONAL IMAGE

Our ability to impress our customers, our clients, and our colleagues can make or break any organization, whether it be a commercial enterprise, a medical practice, or an automobile repair business. If the services that we are providing are of the highest quality and we demonstrate the knowledge and skill that are necessary to assure the public that we are capable of maintaining that quality, then we should do well. However, there are many businesses and other enterprises with personnel who possess the knowledge and skill to provide excellent services, but the businesses do not achieve the level that they are capable of because of the image portrayed by those who provide the services.

How do we achieve the professional image that we would like to have that will put our career or our organization on the fast track to success?

First of all, we must remember that the elements that are incorporated in the process of enhancing our professional life and our professional services involve communication at one of its highest levels!

Here are some other suggestions that, if followed, can assist you in building an excellent image for your business or practice—that is, putting your career on the fast track:

- No matter how bad the day, don't take it out on your clients, your patrons, or your colleagues!

- Be appropriate in all behaviors—no off-color jokes or remarks, no matter how innocent they appear to you.

- Be pleasant. Be a genuinely good person. Be empathetic. Be nice.

- If a client comes to you wanting their money returned or is making some other demand that you may not think is reasonable, think, *If I were the client or the customer, how would I want this handled?*

- Always remember this rule: we are here to serve, not to judge.

- Affirm your commitment to helping people, and show how much you enjoy the opportunity!

- Listen carefully and quietly to what the other person is saying, no matter how urgently you want them to know that you have the solution to their problem!

- When listening, do not interrupt, but reflect on the speaker's feelings through facial expressions and an occasional nod of acknowledgment.

- Be empathetic, but never respond by saying, "I know just how you feel," unless you have clearly experienced what the other person is expressing.

- Maintain good eye contact, but do not stare at the person with whom you are speaking.

- Be likeable. Adopt a positive attitude whether you feel like it or not. In other words, be positive in your daily life at work and at play.

- Watch what you write. Communicate in an appropriate way for the medium in which you are writing: the informal manner that people use in texting is not appropriate for email. Perfect your writing skills (spelling, grammar, punctuation) to impress those with whom you are communicating electronically or by mail.

As Dale Carnegie states in his best-selling book *How to Win Friends and Influence People*, there are four ways and *only* four ways through which we are evaluated by the world (and by those we serve in our professional life): *what we do, how we look, what we say*, and *how we say it*.[18] If we want to influence others in positive ways, those four are important to live by!

THE POWER OF ENTHUSIASM

Napoleon Hill, author of *Think and Grow Rich* and other classics on success, said the following: "Enthusiasm is a state of mind that inspires one to put action into tasks at hand... it bears the same relationship to a human being that steam does to a steam locomotive. It is your vital moving force!"[19]

So, how do we gain the level of enthusiasm necessary to put your career on the fast track?

Here are a few suggestions—

HAVE DREAMS

As Sonny Melendrez says in his talk on "The Unstoppable Power of Enthusiasm," "Your dreams and their outcome serve to confirm the influence of enthusiasm."[20] The real secret to the influence of enthusiasm lies in the imagination: Never stop thinking like a child! Let the child in you come out. If you watch children at play or in the act of "building" something that is a result of their imagination, they do it with enthusiasm, with abandon, and nothing will stop them unless it is a parent who says, "Stop or you'll hurt yourself." We are taught too many times by our parents that enthusiasm should be tempered or there will be negative consequences. We need to get over that mandate and live and work with complete and utter enthusiasm!

SHOW COMMITMENT

Legendary Hall of Fame football coach Vince Lombardi once said, "Most people fail, not because of a lack of desire, but because of a lack of commitment." Commitment enables us to harness our enthusiasm and direct it toward productive ends.

BELIEF

Belief, along with enthusiasm, is the foundation and strongest element of success. When you truly believe in what you envision, it begins to take on a life of its own. What you need for success will begin to appear. The vision of your dream, no matter your level of enthusiasm, can be a lonely experience. Even those closest to you, including your partner, your best friend, and your family, cannot see what you see. Some may discourage you by questioning what your aims are. Even though they may mean well, don't ever give up! In the end, enthusiasm involves the *trust* that <u>you</u> possess the unstoppable power of your dreams and that you can do whatever <u>you</u> set your mind to.

THE POWER OF WISDOM

When I was growing up on our farms, I thought that Slim Elder and A.P. Nichols, our two hired hands, were the wisest men I knew. Their sage advice and insights about life, love, and religion seemed flawless. When I had a question about life or love, they always seemed to have an answer that made sense to me. And now as I look back at the advice I received, I can't help but be thankful. My parents also were always full of good advice, and as I was growing up, I felt their wisdom helped me confirm that the path I was on was sound or it keyed me into opportunities for growth in a different direction.

So, what is wisdom? Who possesses it? How is it learned? How is it expressed? The following characteristics of wise individuals will shed light on these issues:

THEY PUT THINGS IN PERSPECTIVE BEFORE
THEY JUMP TO CONCLUSIONS

They don't act impulsively. They think before they react or speak. They step back and observe. They consider all sides of an issue. They think logically. They ask questions.

THEY DON'T WAIT UNTIL THEY ARE OLDER AND SMARTER

People with the greatest amount of functional wisdom can be much less than 30 years of age since it has been found that the correlation between age and wisdom is nearly zero. Further, research has shown that intelligence accounts for about 2 percent of what we call wisdom. So, it doesn't take age or intelligence to function wisely. It takes perspective and functional logic.

THEY ARE WILLING TO QUESTION RULES

Instead of accepting things as they have always been, wisdom involves asking whether there is a better way of doing things.

THEY ARE GENERALLY OPTIMISTIC IN THEIR OUTLOOK
REGARDING SOLUTIONS TO DIFFICULT PROBLEMS

They demonstrate an atmosphere of calm when they are faced with difficult decisions. They are able to look at problems from several different angles with the assurance that they will find an effective path forward.

In the end, the power of image, enthusiasm, and wisdom are three elements that can put your career or your business on the "fast track" to success. Those three give us the power to lead, to get things done, and to impress our customers or our clients. They can give you the edge that moves you ahead in your career and your life!

CHAPTER 14

How to Resolve Toxic Interpersonal Conflicts

One of the most difficult challenges we face in our professional lives involves the resolution of interpersonal conflict. Conflict resolution, I feel, requires more flexibility and more resilience than any other aspect of human communication. However, it is a form of communication in which every person must at some time or another participate, whether they intend to or not.

Here are a few suggestions that can help in situations in which conflict is evident. None of these require a great deal of effort, but sometimes they do require us to use the greatest amount of poise, charm, and patience that we can muster:

- We must try our best to keep a sense of humor. We do not want to allow the conflict to become more serious than it deserves.

- Shoot for a suitable resolution. Or rather, the goal should be to reach a positive solution. A willingness to give a little and to compromise is frequently the key.

- Communicate clearly and openly. Do not expect others to read your mind. This is true in business relationships and, of course, marriage. Never—never take a cheap shot, no matter how easy it would be! And absolutely no ridiculing!

- Don't make a big deal out of a trivial issue. If we do, we need to ask ourselves, "Why am I doing this? What am I really after here?"

- If we are wrong, it is important to admit it. An apology may be all that it takes to conclude on a positive note what could have been a confrontational moment. Saying, "You know, as I think about it, I may be wrong" can enable you to disengage successfully from a potential conflict. Resolving conflict is impossible if we are unwilling or unable to forgive or to admit that we may have been wrong. It's pointless to hold on to an opinion or an incorrect fact just because we don't want to lose an argument.

- It is important to develop the capacity to recognize and respond to things that matter to the other person. Be sure to give honest and sincere appreciation for the other person's expressed concern or opinions.

- It is equally important to develop the ability to avoid holding grudges.

- We must remember that in working with business associates (and in raising children), *demand* is an ugly word. It makes rational adults (and children) react irrationally. We can, however, have points that are necessarily, and for important reasons, non-negotiable.

- When people are speaking loudly, it is often best for us simply to listen quietly.

Have you ever won an argument? Be honest. Have you ever *really* won an argument?

You may have thought you won, but it is generally that the other person simply gave up or got tired of arguing. So, the only way to get the best of an argument is to avoid it.

Remember, a misunderstanding is never concluded successfully with an argument but rather with tact, diplomacy, and a sincere desire to see the other person's point of view.

If another person seems to be intent on "rubbing you the wrong way" and your first instinct is to retaliate verbally, pause, listen, and think first. Don't say anything that you will later regret. It's much better to avoid a confrontation than to have to apologize later.

More than anything else, it is critically important that we control our temper. If nothing else, we can always promise to study the other person's ideas carefully before responding.

And lastly, it is important to know when to let something go. If we can't come to an agreement, then we can simply agree to disagree and appreciate the other person for their unique perspective.

CHAPTER 15

How to Handle the Fear of Change

*C*hange can be exciting—something new and challenging. On the other hand, it can be fear-inducing—the proverbial fear of the unknown. People tend to remain in dead-end jobs or stop themselves from starting or growing a business because they're afraid of change—afraid of failure if they try something new, afraid of what else will change in their life if they do something different. So, they remain in a job that is not fulfilling and find themselves bored and dreaming of change that will never happen.

Many people feel paralyzed at the thought of changing something that others perceive as key to their identity—their prestigious position at work, their position in the community. They may feel as though they will be losing an important part of their self. So, they end up convincing themselves that status quo is preferable to the risk of striking out in a new direction. How sad that it can happen to those who could make positive change in our world—those who could be happier and more satisfied in their career and in their life!

Change is difficult for everyone. We need to see beyond the fear and see the excitement that can be ours if we embark on something new—something more fulfilling—a new career, a new business, a new relationship.

Lucia Giovannini, a psychologist, author, and speaker who studies how to make meaningful changes in one's life, states that "If we really want to live a life that reflects the best of our possibilities, then we have to be open to change and welcome it as a natural part of our evolution."[21] Life is change and change is life. Don't live with the idea that change is punishment; rather, view it as an opportunity to grow, improve, and learn new things.

Giovannini further suggests that we accept the situation that needs to be changed—an action that requires courage, determination, and honesty. This means accepting the fact that life is working for us and our good, even if at the moment we don't realize it.

Perhaps the greatest fear associated with change is the fear of failure. Sadly, the only way we can avoid that is to do nothing and live as a spectator of those who have made positive change in their lives. Is it better to go after our dreams and encounter difficulties along the way or just to remain trapped in the same mindset and position because we refuse to take a chance on ourselves? Remember, the greatest regret comes from never having tried something important to us, not from trying and not succeeding. Moreover, failure is a useful lesson that can facilitate growth and create new opportunities.

If you struggle with a fear of change, do not allow it to trap you in a life that you don't want. While change can be scary, the real tragedy is living a life that doesn't bring you joy.

CHAPTER 16

How to Lead a Team to Greatness

Leading your team to greatness involves two elements: (1) cultivating the character and personality traits that inspire trust and respect in others and (2) motivating those you are leading to greatness.

QUALITIES OF EFFECTIVE LEADERS

What makes an effective leader in any profession? Can we truly become a leader without becoming someone others look up to?

First of all, leadership isn't about the position one holds. Many people have been assigned leadership positions when they have no reason to be there. Leadership is not a role or a title; it is a posture of service—a way of interacting with others that inspires action and progress in them. It is only after this service orientation has been developed that one should be able to adopt the formal title of "leader."

I've heard people say, "I know a leader when I see one." But then they can't describe what a leader is. Well, if we can't describe leadership, then how will we know a leader when we meet one? More importantly, how will we become leaders ourselves? If you want to make an impact in your organization, your community, or in the broader world, learning what constitutes leadership is critical.

In searching through the literature on leadership, I have found that there are several characteristics that consistently emerge in leaders across professions and industries. Among others, those characteristics include:

- Being respectful

- Being intuitive

- Being an effective and open communicator

- Being a good and willing listener

- Being honest

- Being humble

- Being an innovator

- Giving honest praise and compliments to their team members

- Being interested in serving others rather than themselves

- Being a creative problem-solver

- Inspiring team members by their example

- Taking calculated risks

- Being courageous and firm in their decisions

- Pushing themselves hard for the good of the organization they serve

- Going out of their way to make the organization a fun place to work

- Communicating in an empathetic manner

- Valuing their people and being attuned to their needs

I feel that one reason many so-called "leaders" are distrusted today is that they are seen as self-serving. But to be an effective and respected leader, it is critical that we develop good habits in working with people—I mean *all* those with whom one works with, *all* those whom we serve, not just our inner circle.

That is leadership!

Further, to complement the qualities of effective leadership, one must also have the ability to motivate those they serve.

MOTIVATING OTHERS TO GREATNESS

Motivated team members are generally happier and more productive. How can leaders inspire their teams to feel motivated to do their absolute best? Here are a few ideas:

- Sit down with each team member individually to get to know them. Ask about their goals, their dreams, their aspirations. What is important to them? If they could change any aspect of their work environment, what would it be? Where do they want to be five or ten years down the road? Those are important questions that cause team members to feel valued.

- The leader should ask what motivates their team members. What are their immediate desires and wishes? What would motivate them to remain with the organization on a long-term basis?

- Furthermore, in order to inspire greatness in others, leaders should strive to create a work environment that is open, trusting, and fun. They should encourage new ideas and initiatives.

- Leaders should involve team members in decisions, especially those decisions that directly affect them.

- They should celebrate the successes of the organization, the department, and the individuals in it.

Those who develop into effective leaders and those who learn the art of motivation can be successful in any work or service environment. Neither trait comes naturally. No one is born a leader, nor is one born with the ability to motivate others. Those are traits that must be learned and cultivated. We learn them by being fortunate enough to work or associate with masters of those traits and emulating them as we develop our own qualities of leadership and motivation.

CHAPTER 17

How to Create Deep Customer Loyalty

Although extremely important, the art of communication is not the only important aspect of what we do in our professional life that influences the success of our business and our positive impact on our customers or clients. Our ability to impress our customers with our professionalism, our support, our skill, and our consideration of their needs can make or break our business or hinder our success in any work environment.

Customers or clients who are served by those who make them feel comfortable and respected become repeat customers. Repeat customers tend to spend more money in your business than new customers. A 5 percent customer retention rate can boost profits by 25 to 95 percent. In addition, retaining repeat customers is cheaper than recruiting new ones.

Get to know your customers—their names, the products they buy, and perhaps new products they might like.

Affirm your commitment to serving people, and convey how much you enjoy it!

Play to your strengths—what do you offer that other businesses do not? Include information on certain products that might interest potential customers.

Encourage customer feedback for the purpose of learning their opinion regarding your services and products.

If a customer or client comes to you wanting their money returned or is making some other demand, no matter what the reason, simply smile and comply. Initiate the refund without questioning or inquiry.

If appropriate, use social media to attract customers by providing "behind the scenes" information. But remember that your personal/professional image is the key to defining your reputation. Public perception of you determines to a sizeable degree how successful you and your business will be.

If your clients are receiving excellent service and you are showing them that you are caring, thoughtful, and trustworthy, then they will "sing your praises" to others in your community and your business or organization will continue to grow.

CHAPTER 18

How to Leverage the Power of Creativity to Solve a Problem

We all know people who seem to be able to take a problem that should have a simple solution and then manage to find a very complicated way to solve it, either spending more money than was intended or unnecessarily wasting a great deal of time. On the other hand, we find too few individuals who can take difficult problems and, through their ingenuity and creativity, design solutions that are elegant in their simplicity.

Ingenuity is housed in creativity. Ingenuity is defined as "the quality of being clever, original, and inventive in the process of applying ideas to solve problems, meet challenges, or develop new ideas." In searching for a leader for any organization or business, a person who is creative in problem-solving, who demonstrates ingenuity in designing avenues for moving projects or programs forward in creative ways, even with limited resources, is a valuable find.

Ingenuity—and, I will add, creativity, which ingenuity requires—occurs naturally in children. But as children grow into adulthood, they are often taught to conform to certain adult standards that can stifle creativity. We learn a trade, we are taught according to established rules, and we learn that ingenuity and creativity might be looked at as outside the norm and perhaps not acceptable. A landmark study by George Land tested creativity in 1,600 children ages 5, 10, and 15. Test results measuring degree of creativity for 5-year-olds revealed a score of 98 percent; for 10-year-olds, a score of 30 percent; and for 15-year-olds, a score of 12 percent. The same test given to 28,000 adults revealed a score of 2 percent.[22] Creativity was essentially *gone* by adulthood! If only we could retain the quality that is naturally occurring in children as we mature into adulthood, perhaps we could use our ingenuity—our creativity—to transform our businesses, our schools, our institutions, our churches to likewise become more innovative!

America is known for being a place where innovation and ingenuity are encouraged. History commemorates those who have leveraged their creativity to find unique solutions to common problems. Think for example, of Benjamin Franklin, who, besides being one of our Founding Fathers, discovered electricity and invented bifocal eyeglasses, the lightning rod, the odometer, swim fins, the Franklin stove, and many other devices. George Washington Carver made history in agriculture. He was a botanist, chemist, and an inventor of over 300 products, primarily deriving from peanuts, including dyes, inks, plastics, laundry soap, laxatives, hand lotion, fuel briquettes for heating, and many others. Thomas Edison's ingenuity, of course, made history. He took Benjamin Franklin's discovery of electricity and found a way to use it to light our homes. His many inventions include the incandescent light bulb, the phonograph, the motion picture camera, telegraph products, the alkaline storage battery, and many others. He received 1,093 patents during his lifetime! He was amazing!

Innovation, ingenuity, and creativity have been, and hopefully will remain, an important part of America. When I was in grade school at my small, two-room rural school in the center of Kansas, our teacher taught us to be as creative as our minds would allow. When the lessons of the day for my grade were over, I would have time on my hands to use my creativity. So, with pencil and paper, I designed things that I felt would be helpful to me and to others. I designed a car that would protect its occupants in case of an accident—a head-on collision would not injure those inside of the vehicle. Since I didn't like to make my bed each morning, I designed a device that would make my bed with a single motion of my hand. I designed a robotic lawn mower that would allow me to sit and watch rather than push. I designed a three-foot-tall aluminum solid fuel rocket, and more. Although none of my designs ever reached the U.S. Patent Office, the opportunity to use my creativity, to develop my ingenuity, has helped me throughout my life.

We all possess creativity and ingenuity. We simply must release it. Or, in better terms, we simply need to use it, or we lose it!

CHAPTER 19

How to Make a Difference and Leave a Legacy

*T*his is a brief story about a fellow who has a great position with a prestigious firm but is not advancing in his career because he begins projects that could be great but then discontinues them because he doesn't feel that they would make a significant contribution. He leaves his work partially completed, complaining that he doesn't have the company resources or assistance that he needs to finish them well. His superior is now considering dismissing him from the company due to a lack of constructive contributions. In addition, this man is not contributing at home because he doesn't feel that he has established himself as a valued member of the family.

At this low point in his life, he drifts off to sleep one night and enters into a fitful dream that seems very real to him. In this dream, he goes on a journey to various places in his mind where he might discover the source of his discontent, lack of productivity, and lack of success in his professional and family life. In his dream, he is guided into the spaces he has currently found himself—the "valleys and shadows" of discontent, procrastination, avoidance; the "graveyards" of good intentions, of wonderful ideas that were never fully realized but could have contributed to his field and to the lives of his family and colleagues that may never be realized unless he begins to change.

His journey continues on through his mind until in the end he reaches a vast dark void in which the potential for all of the unfinished aspects of his life, both at work and in his family, are suspended—floating in space, drifting, and waiting to be completed. As he views that dark void and all the unfinished parts of his occupational and family life that are still floating in the darkness, he is drawn toward it. He tries to resist but cannot. He feels as though there is a force pulling him. But then he realizes that he must enter that vast void alone in order to acknowledge and retrieve all that remains unfinished.

In that dream, as he drifts slowly toward that dark void, he hears the voice of his recently deceased uncle—his favorite uncle on whom he had always relied for sound advice as he was growing up—speaking the words he shared from his deathbed: "From now on, it is up to *you*! You have what it takes to be successful! You and I together have prepared you for your life! You have the ability to do whatever you set your mind to. You have the intelligence, the stamina, and the strength to do wonderful things! So get out there in the world and make me proud!"

And he did—as we all can!

CHAPTER 20

How to Build Influence through Praise and Kindness

There is nothing that can boost your success more than a simple act of kindness. Similarly, operating from a general posture of kindness will improve your mood, decrease your stress, and foster strong personal and professional relationships. Here's what kindness tends to do:

Kindness creates positivity. Being kind gives you a natural high, making you feel happier and more positive—more likely to be creative and productive, increase job success, develop healthy relationships, and sustain better health.

Kindness is contagious. Small random acts of kindness passed on from one person to another tend to make connections in and beyond the work environment. They are building blocks of caring, where people feel good about being there rather than disengaged.

Kindness boosts productivity. Kindness creates an environment of respect and caring. The Association of Professional Executives of the Public Service of Canada found that a work environment filled with respect and kindness prompts those who work there to possess more energy, express more satisfaction with their jobs, and be more committed to their organization.[23] In other words, meaningful acts of kindness will lead to more engaged and connected team members and customers.

In order to encourage kindness in yourself and others in your organization, attend to the following practices:

Model kindness. Acknowledging the good work that people do makes them feel appreciated and encourages them to excel each day.

Share positive greetings. Open each day with a "Hello!" or "Good morning!" and close out the day with a "Have a good evening." Doing so helps to create a positive work environment. It lifts the spirit of both the giver and the recipient of the greeting!

Stop rumors. If we hear negative talk or gossip about a fellow team member, no matter how small, it is up to us to stop it rather than letting it go on.

At a time when the day-to-day rush of our lives seems to take over and when many are worried about doing whatever they need to do in order to simply keep their jobs, going out of one's way to show kindness can seem to take a back seat. However, we can be the catalyst that brings a brighter element to the organization with a few simple acts of kindness. We can try being friendly and considerate. Bringing a happy "Good morning!" to our team members in the morning is a simple gesture, and it's not that hard to do!

EPILOGUE

*W*e all want to be successful in our personal and professional life—and we all have the potential to achieve that! We may not become the president of a company or an organization, but not all of us desire to be president. However, we want to do the best we are capable of and to achieve our own level of success.

Earlier in this book I asked the question, "How do we achieve the level of success that we dream of?" The processes involved in enhancing our personal and professional life require *communication* at one of its highest levels. That's because the image that we present to those with whom we associate on a daily basis, including our leaders, our team members, and, importantly, our clients and customers, makes or breaks our career or business. We need to ask ourselves, "Are we the kind of person with whom others want to work and by whom our clients want to be served?" Being that kind of person means being authentic, positive, and polite. It means creating the personal charm that persuades and makes others feel at ease. You then become the person with whom others desire to associate and clients and customers feel comfortable being served by.

This book has provided you with 20 chapters that describe attitudes and actions that will enhance the possibility that you will be successful in your personal and professional life. There are those who are told early in their life that they probably will not be successful during their lifetime, but they rise above that terrible prediction and even become a star in their profession or industry! Albert Einstein was told by his teachers that he would probably not amount to much, but he rose above that prediction and became a celebrated scientist. Thomas Edison found himself with a similar prediction, and a great deal of what we use today is the result of his genius.

No matter where you are, who you are, or what your circumstances are, you can become a success in your personal and professional life! I know you can! You have the potential to become a star!

EPILOGUE

I hope that you enjoyed this book and, as you read it, you discovered avenues for success that perhaps you had not considered before.

Take this book with you and read it again. It could become your ultimate partner for success!

NOTES

1. Jim Stovall, *Wisdom for Winners: A Millionaire Mindset* (Shippensburg, PA: Sound Wisdom, 2014), 11.

2. Sherrie Campbell, *Success Equations: A Path to Living an Emotionally Wealthy Life* (New York: Morgan James Publishing, 2018).

3. Kathy Cuprino, "5 Steps to Speaking Up Powerfully When You Feel You Can't," *Forbes.com*, May 16, 2018, https://www.forbes.com/sites/kathycaprino/2018/05/16/5-steps-to-speaking-up-powerfully-when-you-feel-you-cant/?sh=1d004e3c6517.

4. "Failure Is Success if We Learn from It," *Forbes.com*, n.d., https://www.forbes.com/quotes/6315/.

5. Jim Stovall and Ray H. Hull, *The Art of Influence* (Shippensburg, PA: Sound Wisdom, 2018), 60.

6. Sherrie Campbell, "7 Ways to Master Poise Under Pressure," *Entrepreneur*, June 16, 2016, https://www.entrepreneur.com/article/277556.

7. Carol Kinsey Goman, "The Five C's of Leadership Presence," *CarolKinseyGoman.com*, n.d., https://carolkinseygoman.com/the-five-cs-of-leadership-presence/.

8. Carly Benson, "The Art of Being Consistent to Consistency," *Miracles are Brewing*, September 23, 2015, http://www.miraclesarebrewing.com/the-art-of-being-consistent-to-consistency/.

9. Patrick Allan, "Talent Does Not Decide Whether You Succeed," *Lifehacker*, February 23, 2015, https://lifehacker.com/talent-does-not-decide-whether-you-succeed-1687427688.

10. Jim Stovall, "The Next Big Thing," *Refresh Leadership Blog*, October 7, 2019, http://www.refreshleadership.com/index.php/2019/10/big/.

11. Chris Riotta, "If You Want to Be Successful, Be in the Right Place at the Right Time," *Elite Daily*, March 6, 2015, https://www.elitedaily.com/money /entrepreneurship/seizing-opportunities-takes-more -than-luck/956399.

12. Dan Waldschmidt, "The Key to Success," *Benefits Pro*, August 14, 2014, https://www.benefitspro.com/ 2014/08/14/the-key-to-success/?slreturn=2022002 4164901.

13. David Allen, *Stress-Free Productivity: The Art of Getting Things Done*, updated edition (New York: Penguin, 2015).

14. L. M. Cortina et al., "Incivility in the Workplace: Incidence and Impact," *Journal of Occupational Health* 6, no. 1 (2001): 64–80.

15. S. Chris Edmonds, "Four Steps Proven to Cultivate Workplace Civility," *Forbes*, Forbes Coaches Council, April 14, 2017, https://www.forbes.com/sites/forbes coachescouncil/2017/04/14/four-steps-proven-to -cultivate-workplace-civility/#37f970ba37cf.

16. Eugene Raudsepp, "The Art of Listening Well," *Inc .com*, October 1, 1981, https://www.inc.com/magazine /19811001/33.html.

17. Lisa B. Marshall, "How to Improve Listening Skills," *Quick and Dirty Tips*, August 24, 2012, https://www .quickanddirtytips.com/business-career/public-speak ing/how-to-improve-listening-skills.

18. Dale Carnegie, *How to Win Friends and Influence People* (New York: Gallery Books, 1936).

19. Napoleon Hill, *The Law of Success* (Shippensburg, PA: Sound Wisdom, 2021), 101.

20. Sonny Melendrez, "The Unstoppable Power of Enthusiasm," *Vimeo*, n.d., https://vimeo.com/314316703.

21. Lucia Giovannini, "Overcoming Your Fear of Change in 7 Steps," *Wall Street International Magazine*, December 1, 2016, https://wsimag.com/wellness/22073-overcome -your-fear-of-change-in-7-steps.

22. "Can Creativity Be Taught? Here's What the Research Says," *Creativity at Work*, n.d., https://www.creativityat work.com/can-creativity-be-taught/.

23. Lynne Levy, "5 Reasons Kindness Matters at Work," *Workhuman*, November 13, 2020, https://www.work human.com/resources/globoforce-blog/5-reasons-kind ness-matters-at-work.

ABOUT THE AUTHOR

Ray H. Hull is sought after as a speaker/presenter on the topic of "The Art of Communication in Professional Life" and has authored and presented over 700 presentations and workshops across the United States, Canada, South America, and Europe on that and other topics.

He is the author of 28 books, 22 of which are well-established textbooks on "the art of communication in professional life," "communication in aging," "hearing in aging," "hearing rehabilitation," among others. Four others are coauthored with *New York Times* best-selling author Jim Stovall, and two are novels entitled *A Place Called Eden* and *Cloud County*.

He is also a columnist, narrator for the Smithsonian Institution, and a motivational speaker.

Dr. Hull is the recipient of numerous honors and awards. He was elected Fellow of the American Speech-Language-Hearing Association and Fellow of the American Academy of Audiology. He was awarded the Red River Award by the Manitoba Ministry of Health and the Winnipeg League for the Hard of Hearing for significant service on behalf of hearing-impaired adults.

He was named Distinguished Pioneer in Gerontology by the Colorado Gerontological Society. He was awarded the Public Health Service Award for significant public health research and service to the United States. He was also named Distinguished Scholar of the College of Health and Human Services, University of Northern Colorado, on three different occasions. He was awarded the Faculty Achievement Award in the College of Health and Human Sciences at the University of Northern Colorado for outstanding scholarly activity and teaching excellence on three different occasions. He was also awarded the Award of Excellence for Outstanding Public Leadership in the Cause of Better Hearing and Speech by President Ronald Reagan.

He received the Distinguished Professor Award at Wichita State University by the university chapter of Mortar Board, the College of Education Teaching Award for Excellence in Teaching, and the Emery Lindquist Faculty Award for Scholarship and Teaching. He was awarded the 2001 and the 2006 Professor Incentive Award at Wichita State University.

In 2002, 2003, 2004, 2005, 2007, 2010, and 2014, he was named to Who's Who among America's Educators. In 2010, he received the President's Distinguished Service Award at Wichita State University. He received the Delores and Sydney Rodenberg Award for Excellence in Teaching from the College of Health Professions at Wichita State University in 2016.

Dr. Hull holds a B.A. in Forensics, Drama, and Mass Communication from McPherson College, an M.A. in Communication and Disorders of Communication from the University of South Dakota, and a Ph.D. in Human Neurosciences/Audiology from the University of Denver.